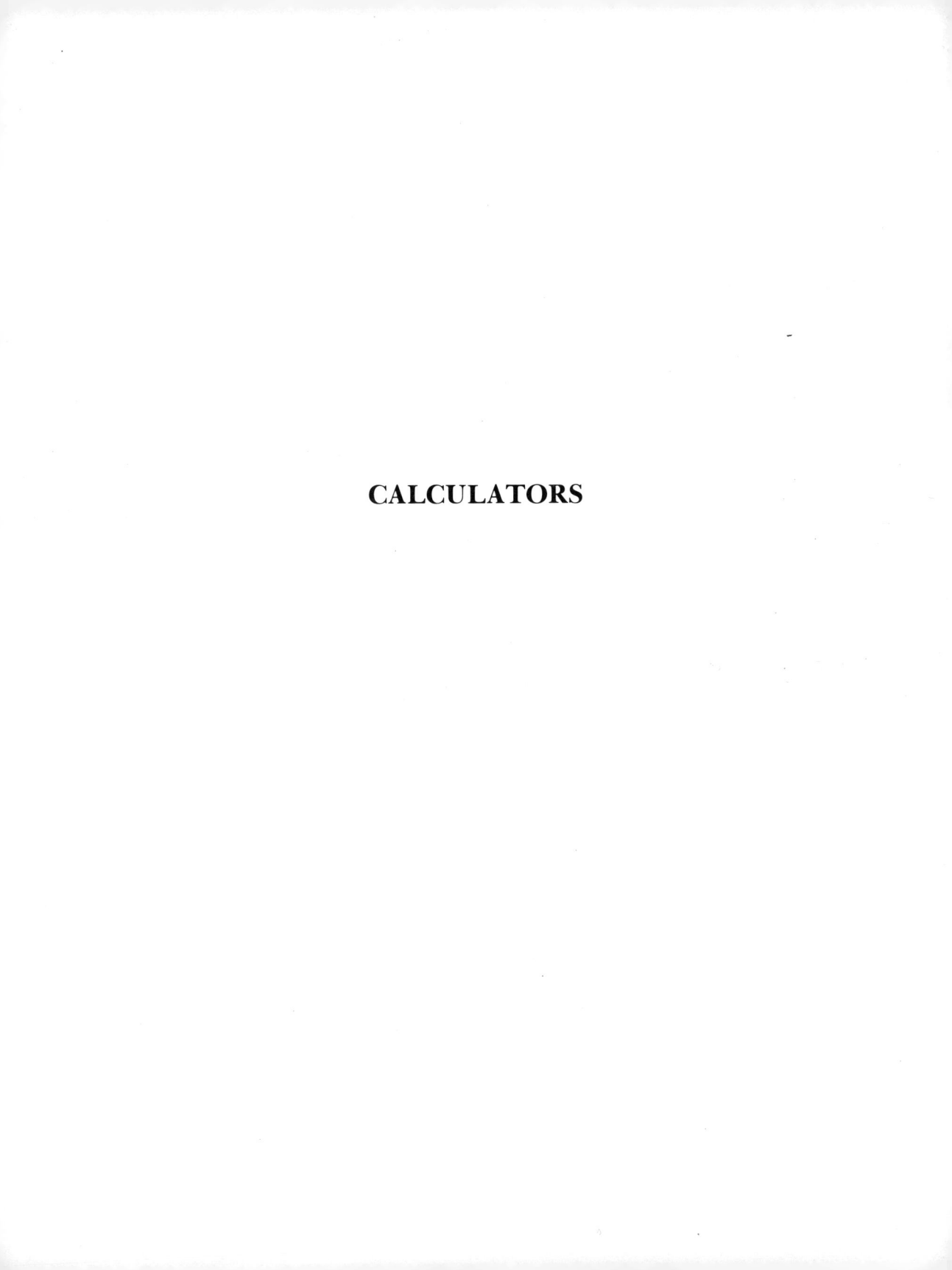

CALCULATORS

Copyright © 1985, Raintree Publishers Inc.

All rights reserved. No part of this book may be reproduced or utilized in any form or by any means, electronic or mechanical, including photocopying, recording, or by any information storage and retrieval system, without permission in writing from the Publisher. Inquiries should be addressed to Raintree Publishers Inc., 330 East Kilbourn Avenue, Milwaukee, Wisconsin 53202.

Library of Congress Number: 84-9791

1 2 3 4 5 6 7 8 9 0 88 87 86 85 84

Library of Congress Cataloging in Publication Data

Haney, Jan P.
   A look inside calculators.

   Includes index.
   Summary: Explains how the parts of a simple calculator work together to display, add, subtract, multiply, and divide.
     1. Calculating-machines—Juvenile literature.
(1. Calculating machines. 2. Mathematical instruments.
3. Office equipment and supplies) I. Frank, Ken.
II. Title
QA75.H317   1984   510'.285'4   84-9791
ISBN 0-8172-1407-0 (lib. bdg.)

CALCULATORS

By Jan P. Haney

CONTENTS
FROM ABACUS TO COMPUTER	5
THE ELECTRONIC CALCULATOR	11
HOW CALCULATORS ADD	23
OTHER KINDS OF PROBLEMS	37
PLAYING WITH NUMBERS	41
GLOSSARY	46
INDEX	47

RAINTREE PUBLISHERS
Milwaukee • Toronto • Mexico City • Melbourne

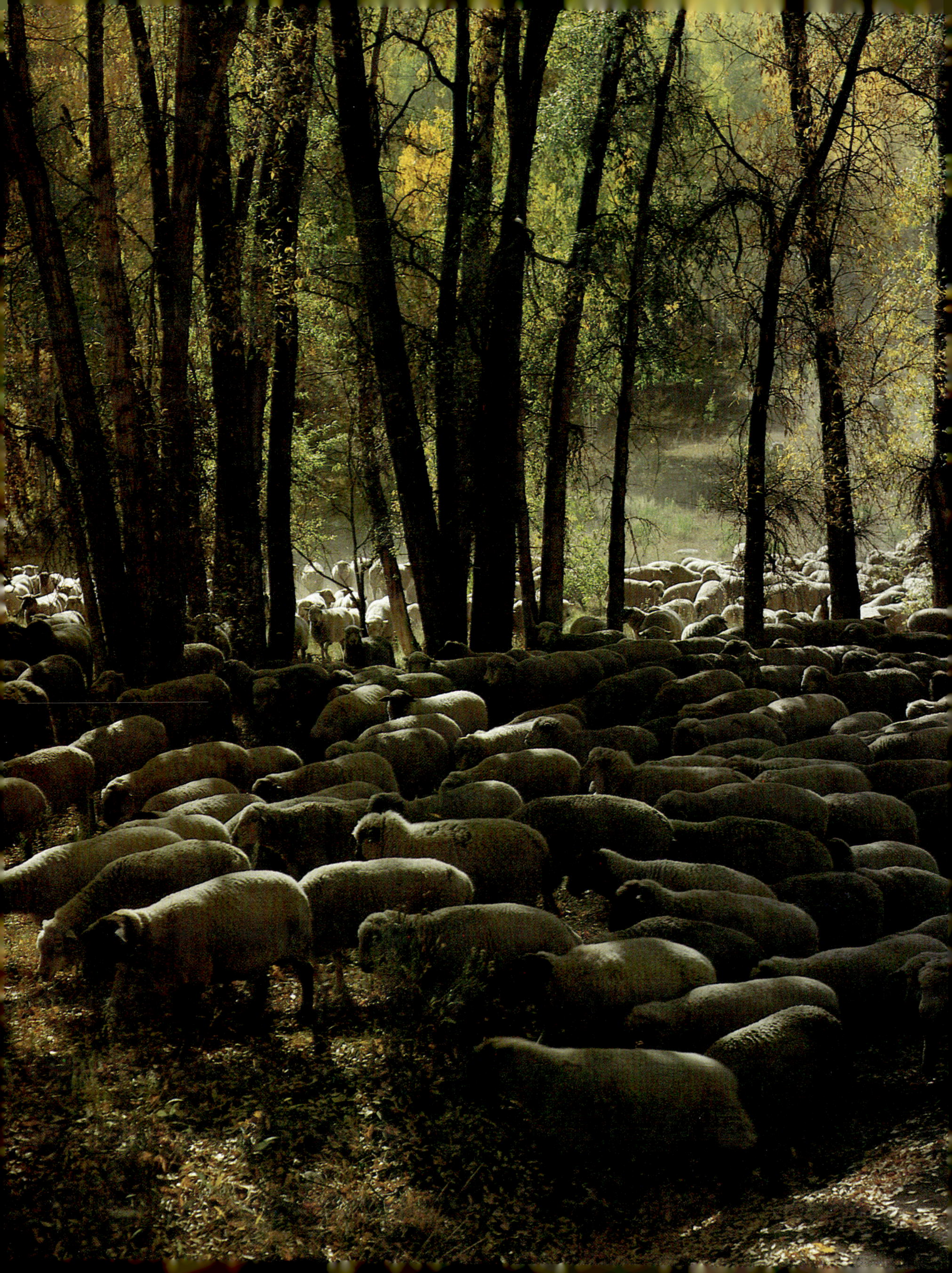

FROM ABACUS TO COMPUTER

Not long ago we only read about small calculators in stories. Now we use them every day at work, at home, and at school. They help make our math quick, easy, and accurate.

Why were calculators invented? How do they work problems so quickly? What happens inside when you press the keys? You may have asked these questions yourself, and this book can help you find the answers. But first, let's see how people handled mathematics before they had these marvelous machines.

Long, long ago, people found that they needed a way to keep track of things. For example, they wanted to know how many days it took for grain to grow. They wanted to know how many sheep were in their flocks. So, very early, counting was invented.

At first, stones were used for counting and keeping track of things. Shepherds let one pebble stand for each sheep in the flock. This was a simple way to keep track of births, sales, and other changes in the flock.

This picture shows an ancient Chinese abacus. Abacuses were first used thousands of years ago in Asia, Greece, and Rome.

As mathematics grew, people began looking for other things to help them with arithmetic. About 5,000 years ago, people learned to string pebbles or beads on a frame. This became the first calculating device. It is called an abacus.

Very slowly, other calculating tools were developed. In 1614 John Napier showed how to do multiplication and division

6

This engraving shows Blaise Pascal (inset) and the "adding machine" he invented.

quickly. He used "rods" that were marked in special ways. These rods were carved out of ivory, and are called Napier's Bones. They were the first slide rule.

The first real "adding machine" was invented in 1642 by Blaise Pascal. It had many gears, wheels, and windows. Later, more complex whirling and whizzing mechanical machines were developed. They had buttons, wheels, and hand cranks.

7

This is Hollerith's electric calculating machine. The inset on the right is the actual picture that was submitted to the U.S. Patent Office in 1892.

In 1890, an American named Herman Hollerith used electricity to run a calculating machine that used punched cards for counting and computing. He was one of the first developers of the modern computer.

By 1950 computers could do all kinds of mathematics. They had many small parts and could work complicated problems very quickly. But they were also very big and expensive. Only very large companies could afford their own computers.

On the right is a section of one of the large computers that were common in the 1950s.

Free Lance Photographers Guild

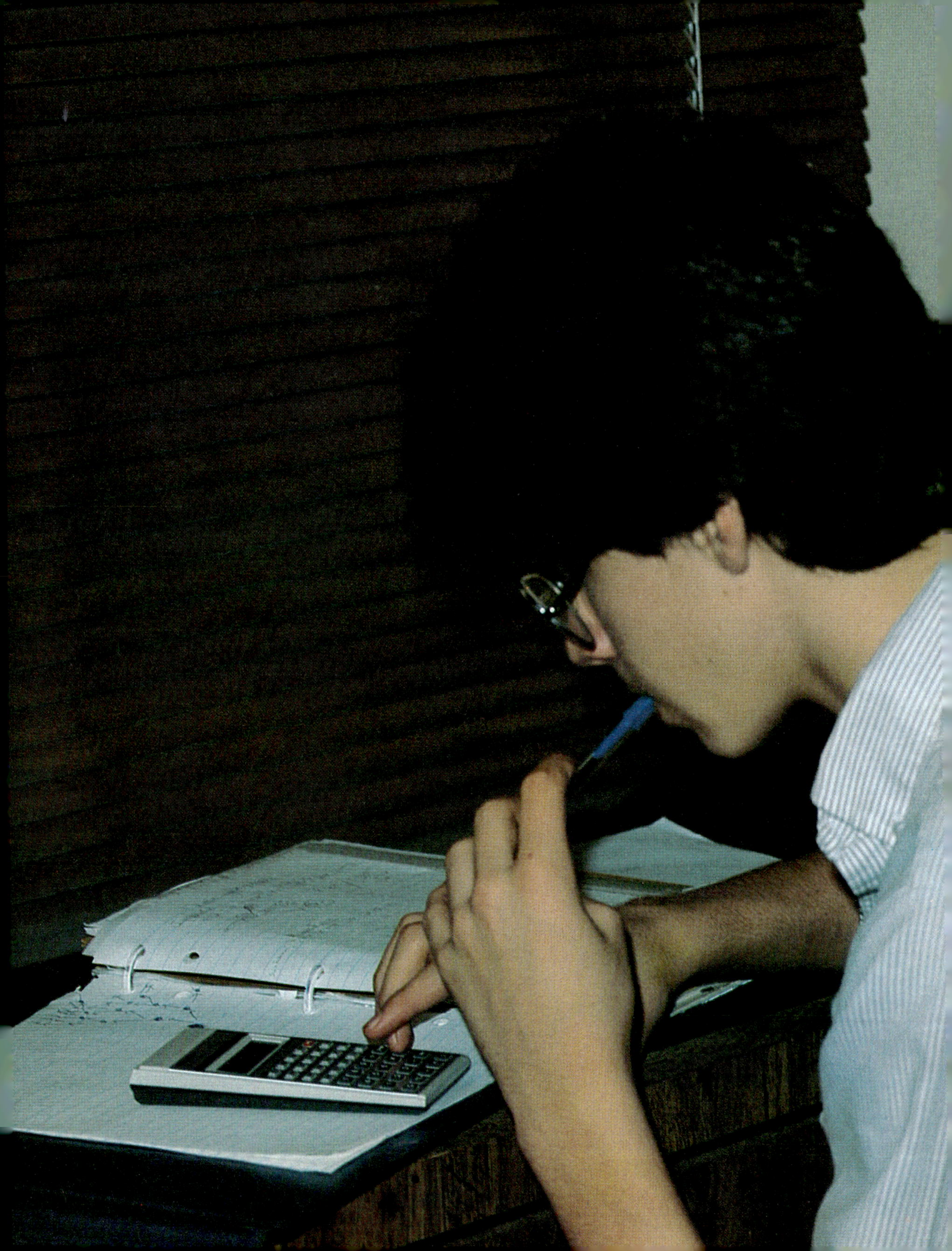

THE ELECTRONIC CALCULATOR

Imagine the excitement a few years ago when people discovered how to build a small, simple calculator that anyone could own and use. People all over the world now enjoy using handheld calculators. Everyday-arithmetic can be done in an instant.

The outside of the calculator looks very simple. There are some keys and a small window. The group of keys is called the *keyboard*. Pressing the keys tells the calculator which numbers to use and what kind of problem to work. The small window near the top is called the *display*. When you press a number key, you'll see that number in the display. The calculator also shows you answers to problems in the display. Most small calculators get power from a battery, but some also plug into walls.

Have you every wondered what makes the calculator work? Numbers and answers appear so quickly that it seems like magic. Let's try a problem. If you have a calculator, turn it on. Let's add 3 and 5. First, press the 3 key.

11

Watch what happens. A number 3 appears in the display.

What made this 3 appear? Pressing the ③ key sent some special information into the calculator. This information said, "The ③ key has been pressed. Remember number 3." Somewhere inside, something remembers the 3 and also makes it light up in the display.

Next press the ⊞ key. This tells the machine to add. Now press the ⑤ key. What happened? The 3 was replaced in the display by a 5. Where did the 3 go? Is the calculator remembering the 3 and your directions to add? Next press the ⊟ key to find out. An 8 is now in the display. What inside the calculator figured out this answer? What happened to the 5 and the 3? Let's look inside and find out.

Here's what the inside of a calculator looks like.

Morley Johnson

These are photographs of the inside of the calculator shown on page 12. Above is the entire inside of the calculator. Below is a close-up of the integrated circuit.

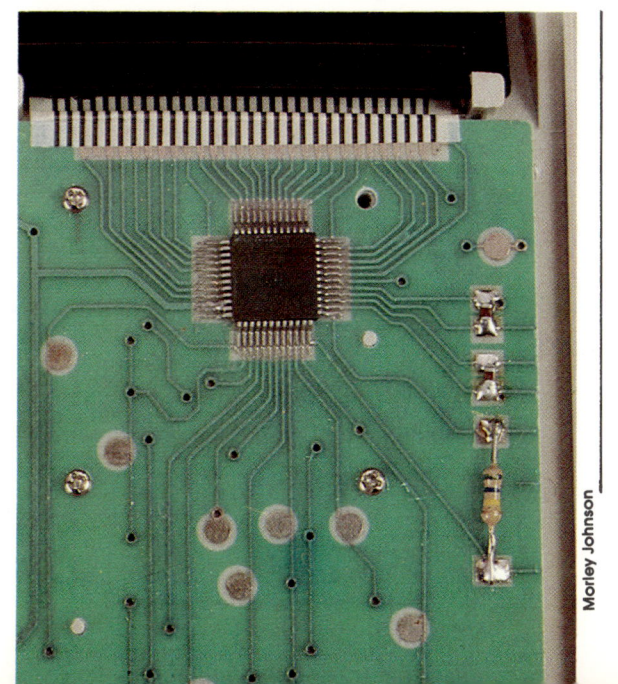

Are you surprised to see so few parts? Doesn't it look simple? Look carefully at each of the parts.

The printed circuit board holds an integrated circuit, the display, and circuit paths (or printed circuits).

13

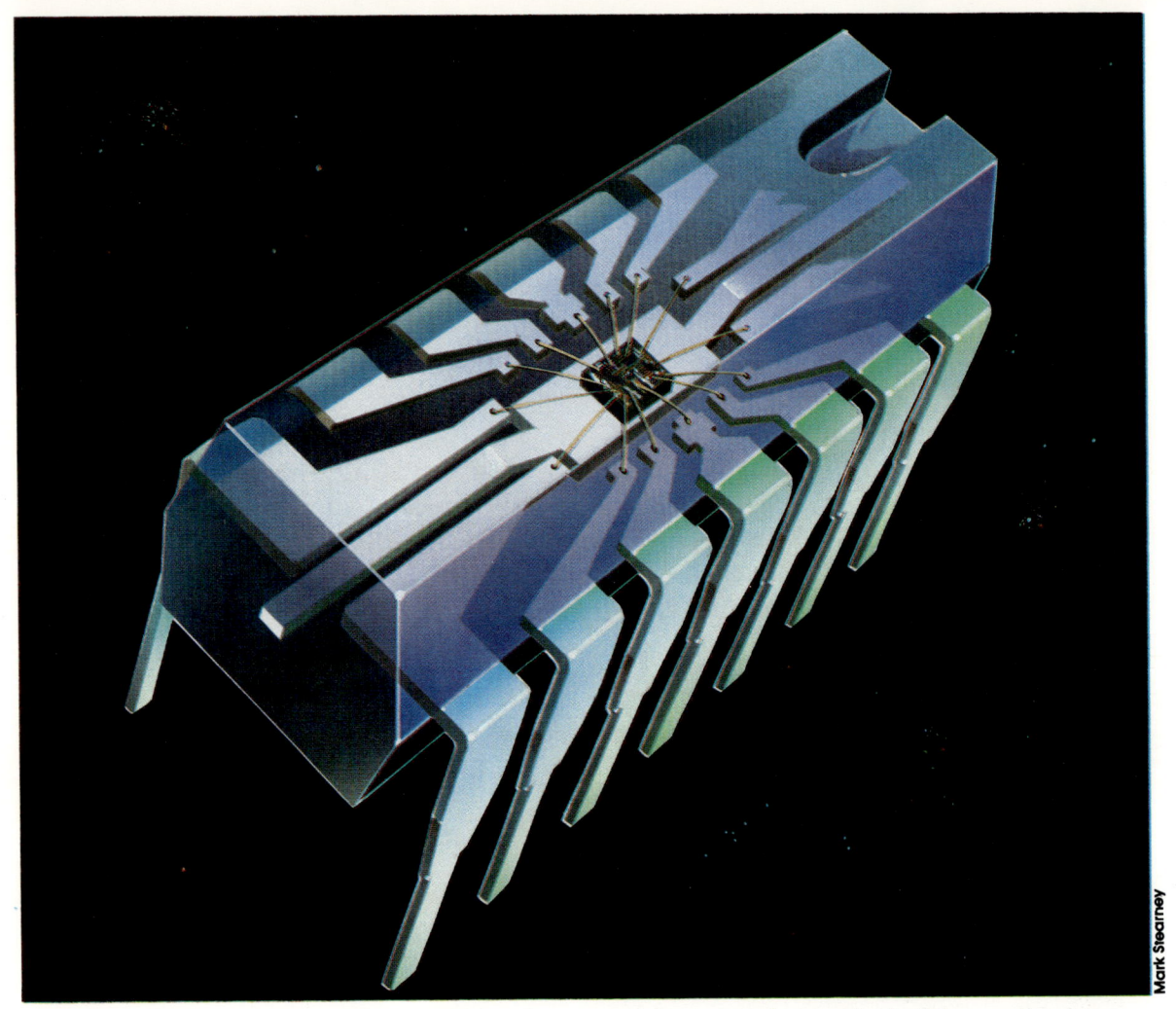

This is an integrated circuit. The metal pins that extend down are the terminals. The small square in the center is the silicon chip.

THE INTEGRATED CIRCUIT

The *integrated circuit* (IC), is a very small (but important) part inside the calculator. What does "integrated circuit" mean? Integrate means "to bring parts together in one place." A circuit is a "path that goes around something." In electricity, a "circuit" is the path of the electric current. An integrated circuit in a calculator gathers many paths of electricity in one place.

The invention of the integrated circuit was very important.

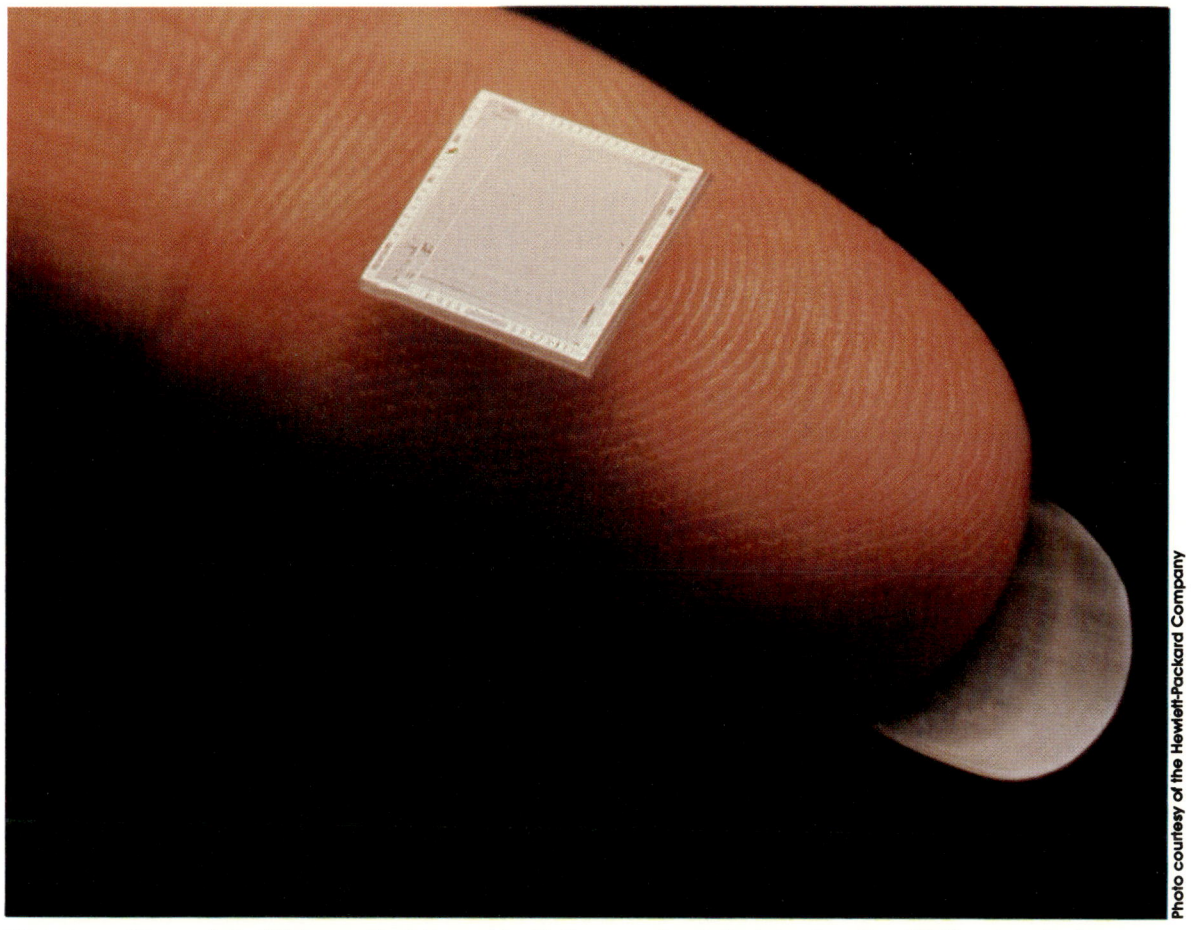

This is a silicon chip. This small chip can hold thousands of electric circuits. All the circuits in a calculator gather in a single chip like this one.

Because of the integrated circuit, large computers could be made small enough to fit in the hand. Inside each integrated circuit are many small circuit paths that were very large in the first computers.

An integrated circuit looks like a small bug with thin metal pins for legs. These pins are called *terminals*. (A terminal is a place where things come in or go out.) Electricity comes in and goes out of the integrated circuit through the terminals.

Inside the integrated circuit, the terminals are joined to a tiny, thin "chip" of *silicon*. Silicon is a very hard, metallike material. The chip is only about the size of a baby's fingernail. This very small chip holds all the electronics that run the calculator. Look at the picture. It is enlarged many times so you can see how tightly the parts on a chip are packed.

This tiny chip is the brain of a calculator. It works something like your brain. The chip controls

This is a photograph of a silicon chip from a calculator. The photo has been enlarged hundreds of times and gives an indication of how complex these tiny chips are.

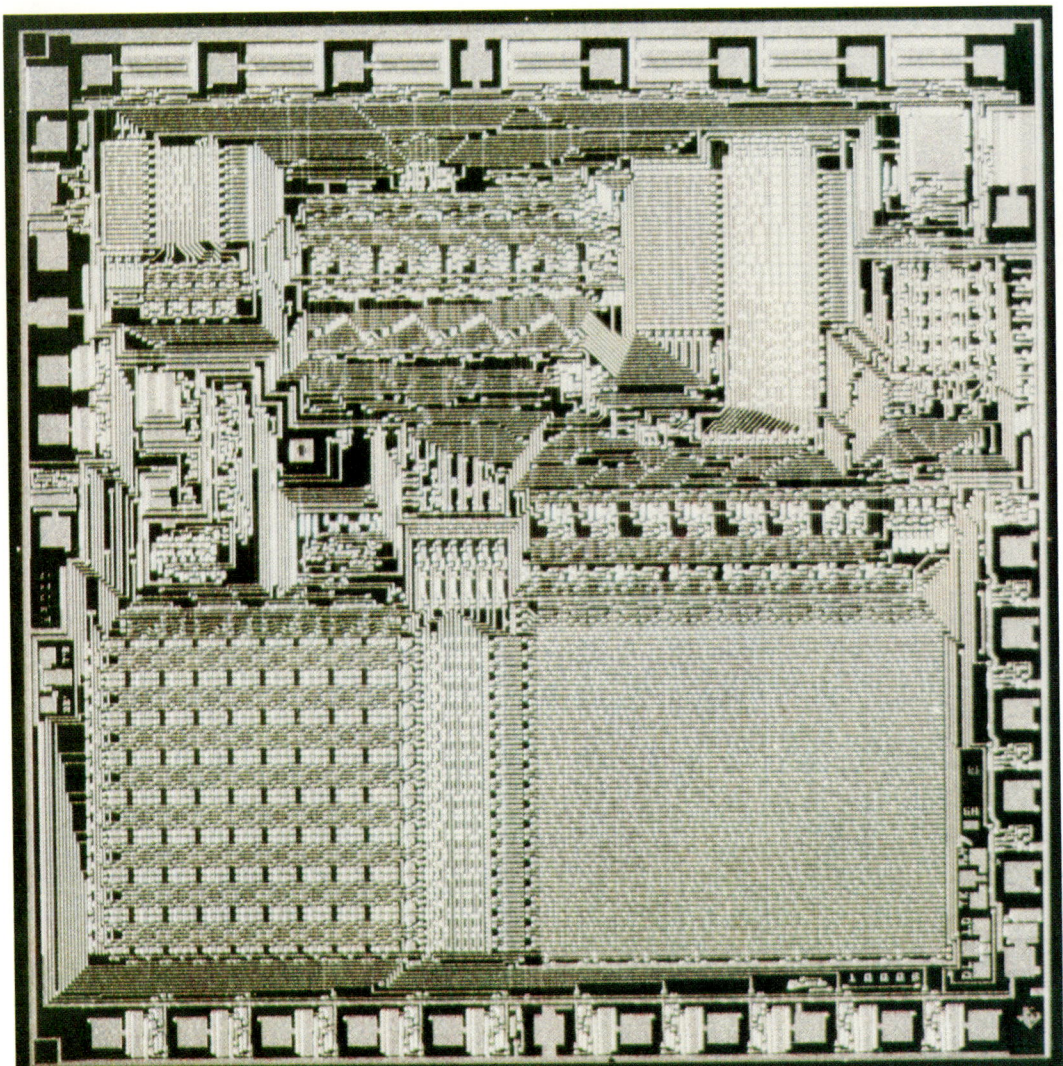

everything. It remembers the information you enter into the calculator. It works out the problems and operates the display. In order to do all these jobs, each job is broken down into small steps. And each step is handled inside the chip in a certain order.

The integrated circuit has many parts. Every part has a job. Look again at the picture of the integrated circuit. Let's learn about all the parts.

Hundreds of chips are built-up on this large silicon wafer. The cutting instrument divides the wafer into individual chips, which are then used in calculators and other electronic devices.

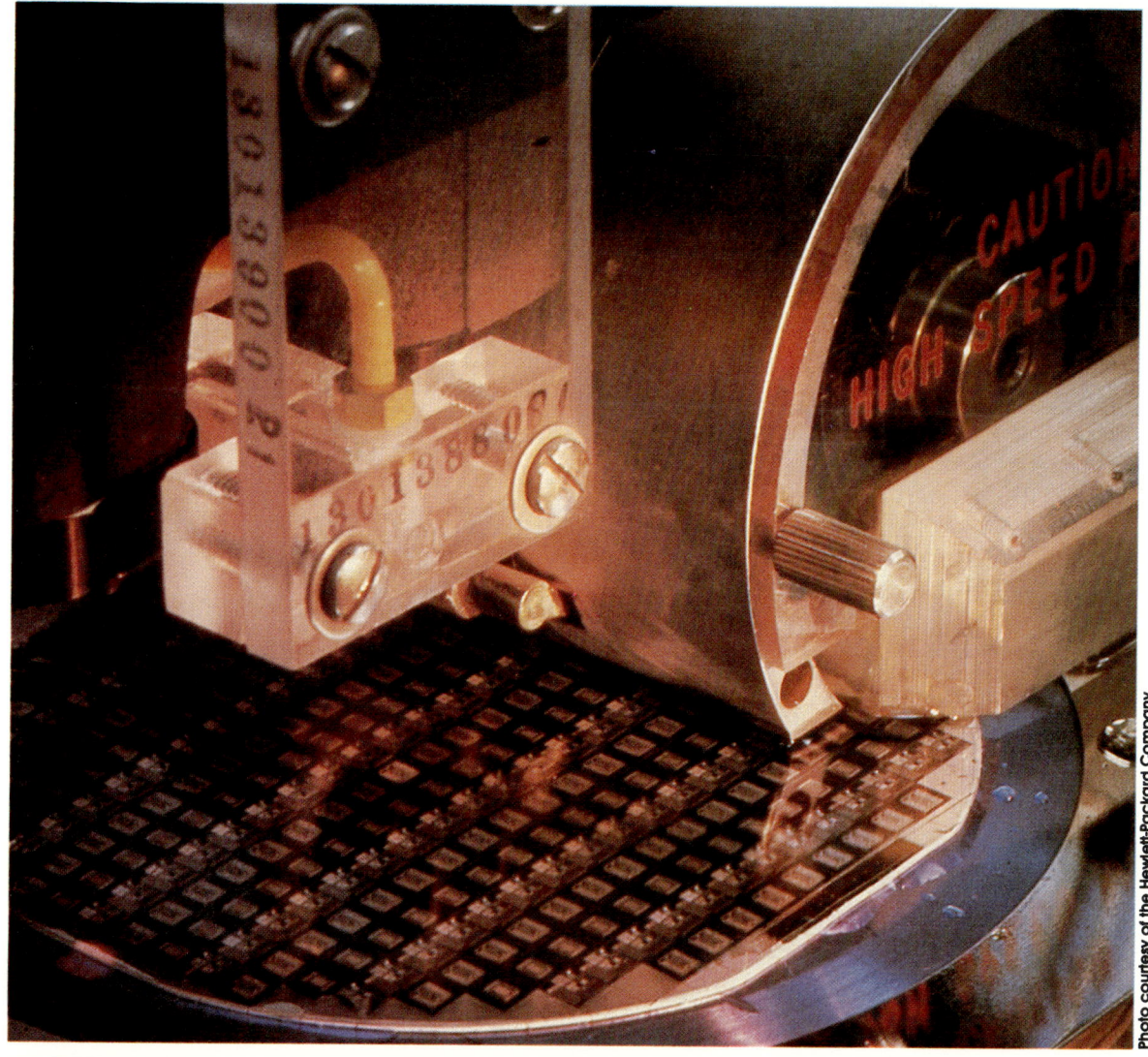

Display

Keyboard

Controller

Instruction
Messengers

Sorgel Studios

The parts of the integrated circuit are all linked to one important part. It is called the *controller*. The controller controls most of what goes on inside the integrated circuit. Instructions and messages whiz to the controller. Then the controller quickly sends the instructions and messages to the other parts. It tells the parts what to do. Imagine that the controller is a robot traffic director. It stays in one place and makes sure that all instructions and messages pass through the integrated circuit in the correct order. As long as the controller is on the job, messages can't "crash" into each other or get out of the line of traffic.

The integrated circuit is such a busy place that the controller can't do this whole job alone. It uses "messengers" to find out what's going on. These messengers are really fast-moving pulses of electric current. The messengers report back to the controller. Then, other messengers take instructions to the rest of the calculator.

Each messenger has a special job to do inside the integrated circuit. One special messenger is in charge of giving instructions to the controller. These instructions tell the controller exactly what needs to be done. Let's call this messenger the *instruction messenger*. This messenger works "behind the scenes," and it doesn't like to be forgotten. So, as we go along, remember the instruction messenger is right there working, too.

ICs are manufactured in a clean environment to keep them free of dust and dirt.

19

Lookout messengers carefully watch the keyboard all the time. By working together, they tell the controller exactly which key you've pressed.

Another important messenger tells the display when to light up and show a number. It is the *display messenger*.

Other messengers have the job of taking care of the memory part of the integrated circuit. The memory part is like a group of little boxes. These memory boxes are used to remember and save numbers. The *memory-box messengers* move numbers in and out of the boxes for the controller.

All of these messengers must do their jobs in a certain order and at a certain time. To make sure the messengers do the right job at the right time, the controller uses a "clock" to time everything. It can't allow a traffic jam in the integrated circuit. Now, let's see how all the messengers work together to solve a problem.

This diagram shows what happens when the controller receives a message from the keyboard of a calculator.

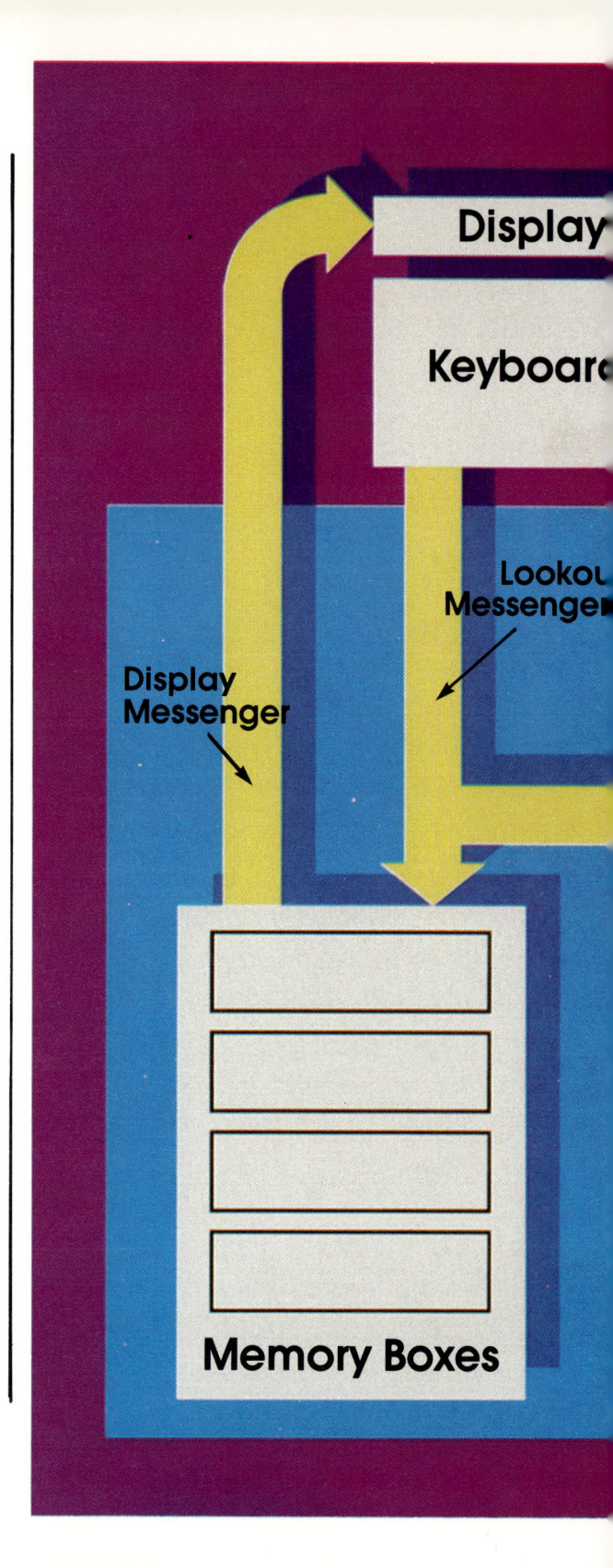

Scan Generator

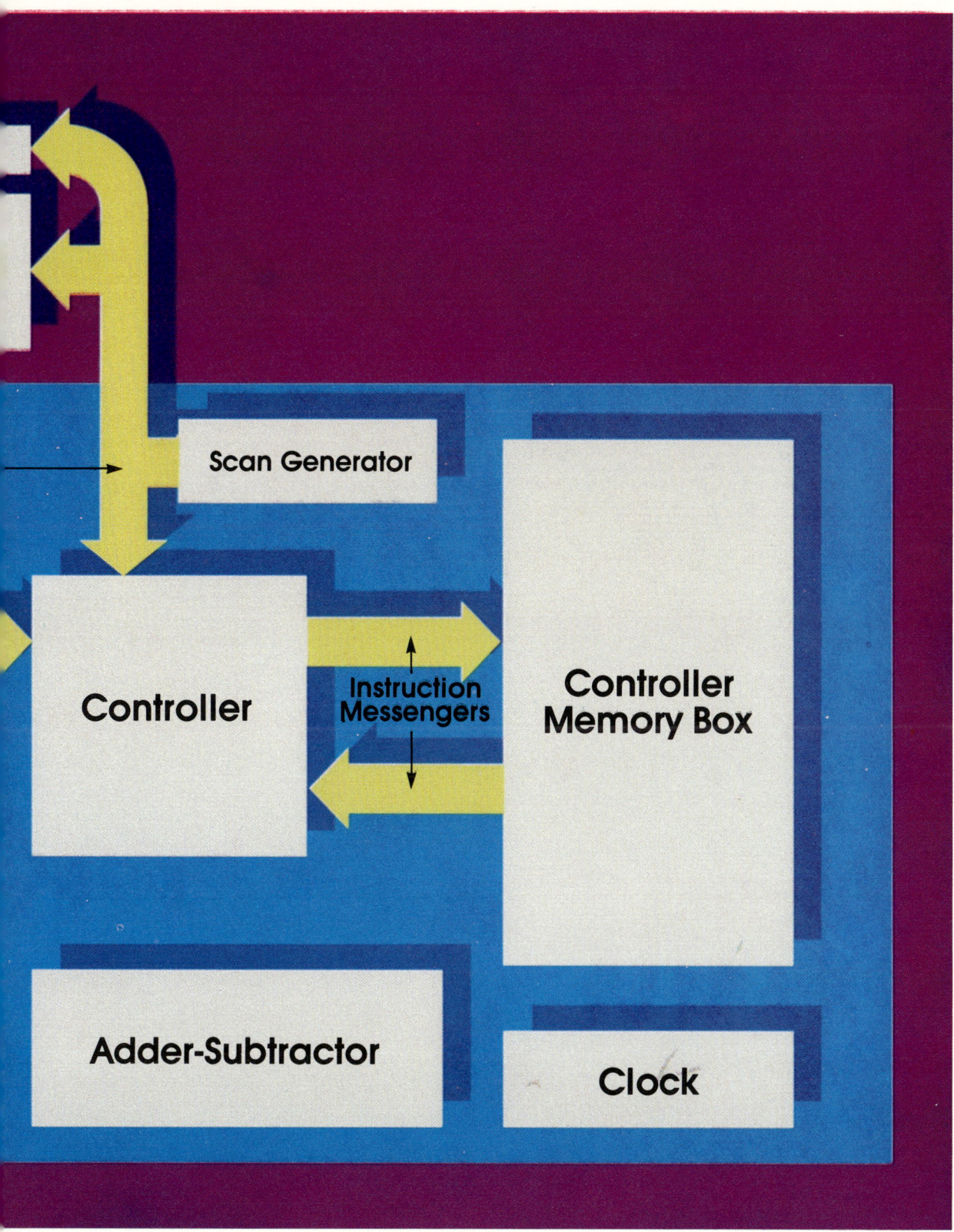

Controller

Instruction Messengers

Controller Memory Box

Adder-Subtractor

Clock

TEXAS INSTRUMENTS
TI-57 LCD
Programmable
Constant Memory
TEXAS INSTRUMENTS TI-5020
TI-30 SLR
Light Powered
TI-66 PROGRAMMABLE
TI-5008

HOW CALCULATORS ADD

Look at the problem 3 + 5 again. What happens in the calculator to work this problem? First, turn the calculator on, if you have one. When the calculator goes on, the controller first sends the memory-box messengers to clear out any numbers that may be in the memory storage boxes. A display messenger then runs to tell the display to light up a 0.

The lookout messengers are keeping a sharp eye on the keyboard. Every time the clock says it's time check the keyboard, they must tell the controller what's going on. Since a key has not yet been pressed, the messengers tell the controller, "No key has been pressed."

Now press the 3 key. The lookout messengers quickly tell the controller, "A key has been pressed. The key is number 3." Once the controller gets a message from the lookouts, the controller is ready to take some action.

After the controller gets the message that a key was pressed, it checks a special memory box for

23

notes. The controller is a very busy "robot." So it must write notes to itself and put these notes in a special memory box. Each time a key is pressed, it checks this box. The notes in the box remind the controller what needs to be done.

Is the ③ key the first key pressed? Yes, it is. The controller writes a note and puts it in the memory box. The note says, "The first number key of a problem has been pressed."

Now, the controller sends the display messenger to tell the display to light up a 3. Also, a memory-box messenger saves the 3 in the display memory box.

Next, press the ⊞ key. The lookout messengers are still checking the keyboard. They take a message to the controller. The message says, "A key has been pressed. This key means 'add'."

The controller now writes a note saying the ⊞ key has been pressed. It must remember to add when the next number key is pressed. The controller then puts the note in the memory box.

The controller knows it must get ready for the next number key. First, it must make sure the 3 is saved. Memory messengers move the 3 to a "waiting" memory box. The 3 "waits" there so the next number can go into the display.

Now press the ⑤ key. The lookout messengers are still working. Again, the message is sped to the controller. The controller checks its notes. The notes remind it that a 3 and a + have been pressed. The controller sends one messenger to save the 5 in the first memory box. And the display messenger carries the news, "Light up the 5 in the display."

The last key we'll need to press for this problem is the ⊟ key. The lookout messengers immediately tell the controller the ⊟ key has been pressed. The controller knows this key means "the end of the problem." It's time to scurry. The messengers take copies of both the numbers and also the "add" instruction out of the memory boxes. The controller directs the messengers to take

These diagrams show the four main steps a calculator goes through to do the problem 3 + 5.

24

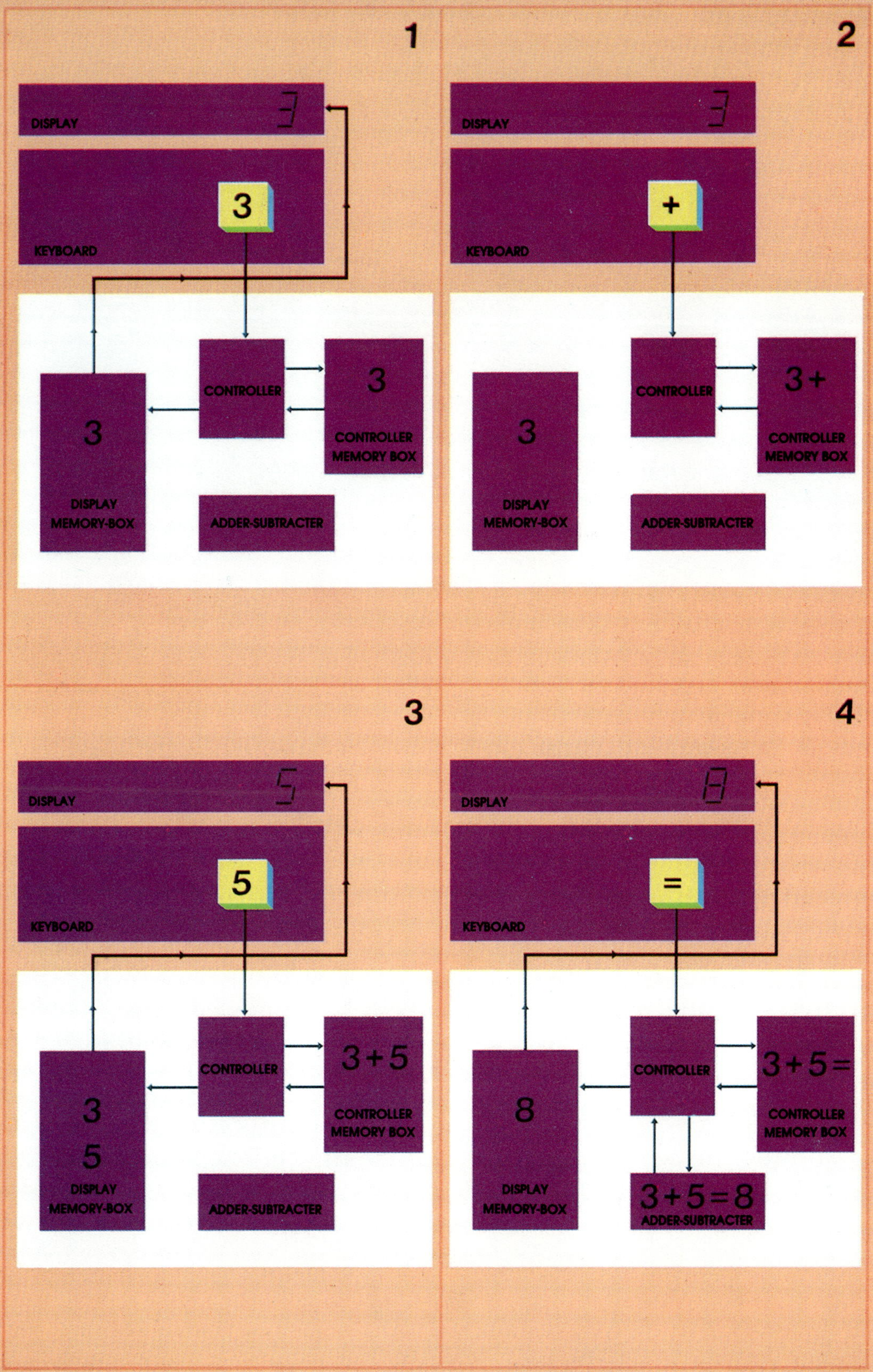

Sorgel Studios

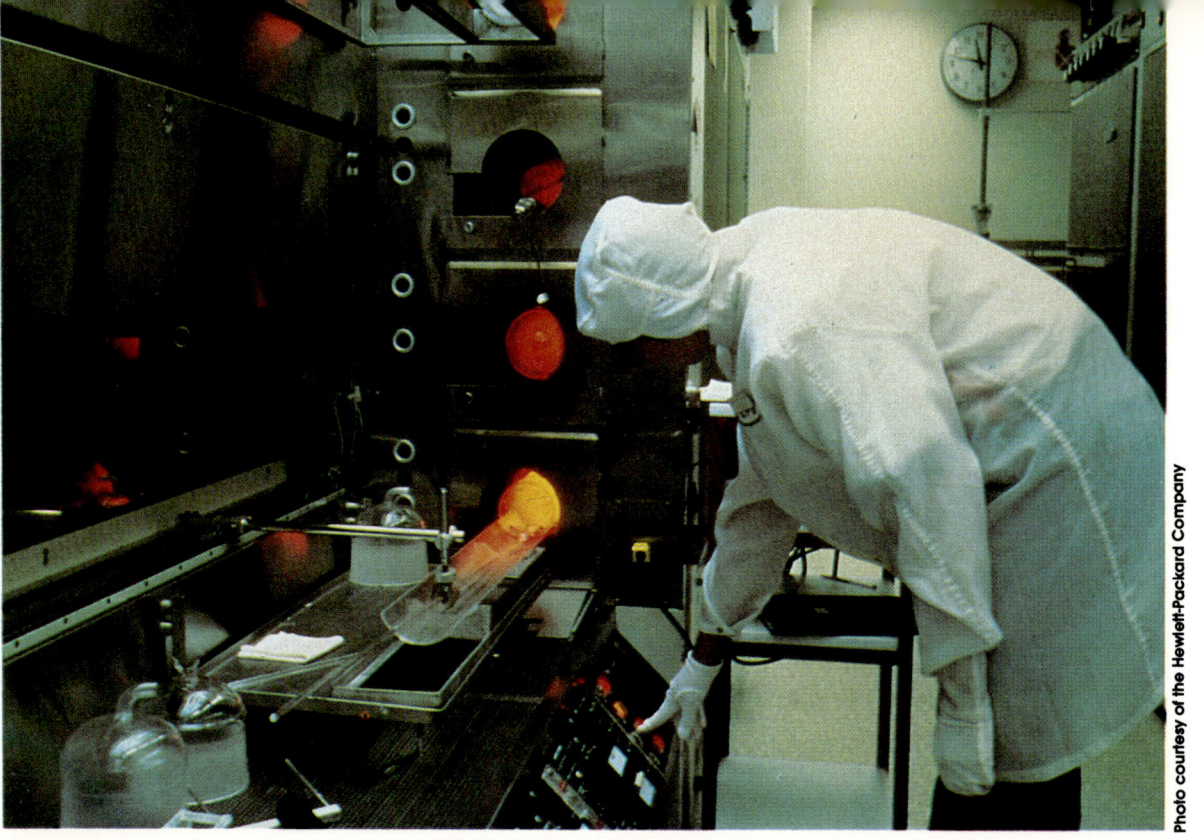

Integrated circuits are fabricated on round wafers and are then given a chemical treatment in oven-like chambers.

copies of the 3 and the 5 and the + to another place. This place is called the *adder-subtracter*.

The adder-subtracter does all the arithmetic in the calculator. When it finishes, it sends the answer back to the controller. Then the controller sends the memory-box messengers out once more. One messenger puts the answer, 8, in the *answer memory box*. Another messenger, the display messenger, tells the display to light up an 8.

The problem is finished.

It takes some time for us to talk and think about everything that is going on in the integrated circuit. But the controller and its helpers haven't slowed down. All of this happened almost as fast as the keys were pressed.

As we said before, the messengers sent by the controller are really tiny pulses of electrical current. Let's see how these electrical pulses work with other parts of the calculator.

THE DISPLAY

Press the 3, 4, 8 keys. Then look closely at the lighted numbers in the display. You will see that each number is made up of small lighted pieces. These pieces are called segments. The 1 has two segments. The 4 has four segments. And the 8 has seven segments. Each number in the display has seven segments. Any of the numbers, 0 through 9, are formed by lighting two or more of the segments. An eighth segment in each number position shows a decimal point.

Some calculators have a ninth segment in the display. The ninth segment can hold a minus sign, so you can use negative numbers. Look at the drawing of the seven segments. Which segments light up to make the number 2? (Did you choose a, b, g, e, and d?) Which segments light up to make the other numbers?

This photograph shows the segments that form numbers in a calculator.

Photo courtesy of the Hewlett-Packard Company

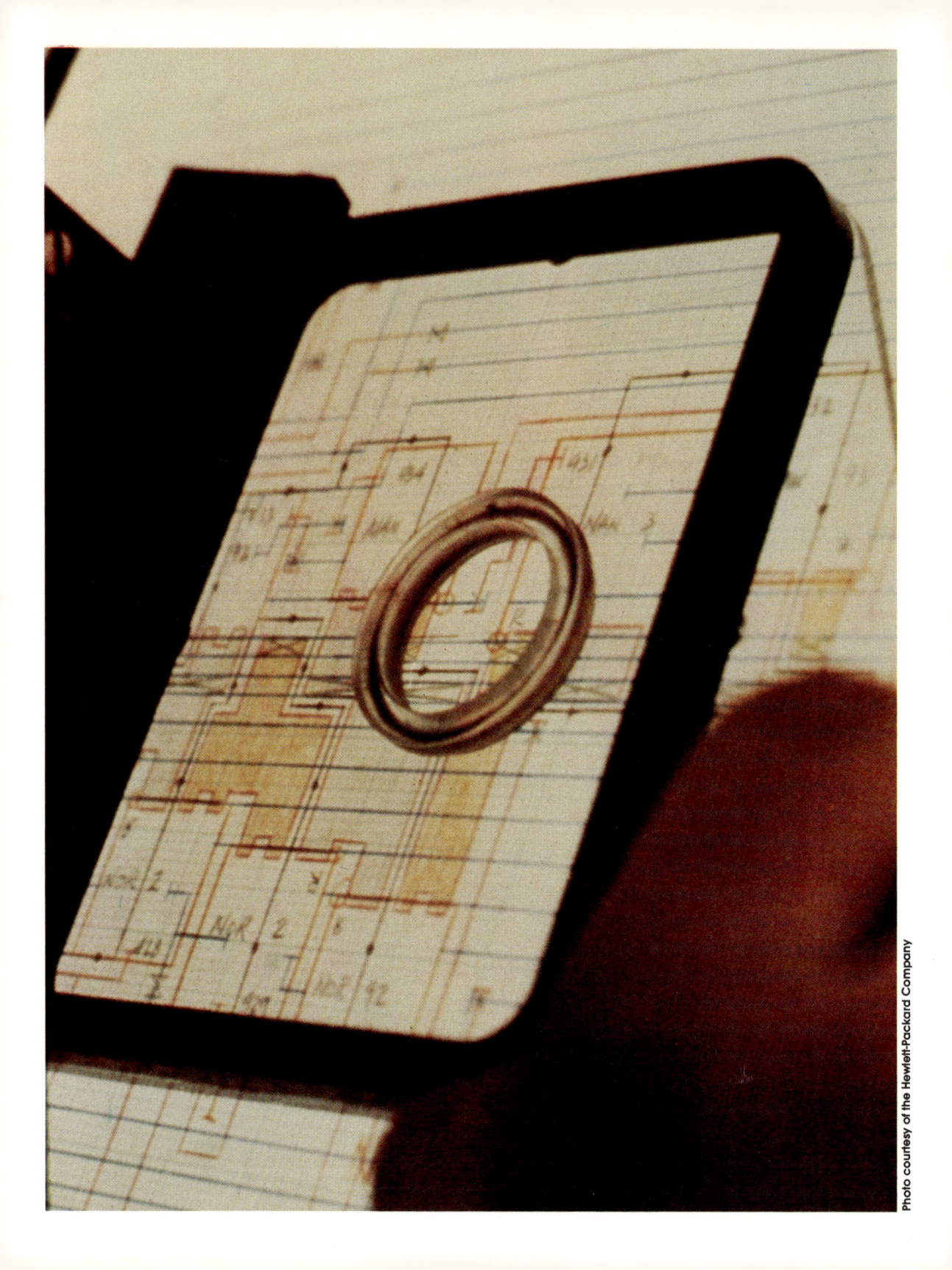

OTHER PARTS OF THE CALCULATOR

Some other important parts are the wires (or circuits) that carry electric current through the calculator. Actually, the wires in a calculator are not really wires. They are very thin lines of metal. The lines are etched on the calculator chip by laser beam or X-ray. Thousands of these "wires" can fit on one small chip. Some of these wires connect the keyboard to the printed circuit board. Other wires are on the printed circuit board. The names of these parts sometimes tell what the parts do. Here are the parts we'll talk about.
- segment lines
- scan lines
- keyboard input lines

The *segment lines* carry electricity from the power supply through the segments in each number position in the display. They light up the segments to show the numbers.

Scan lines "scan" the keyboard. They look for signals coming from the keyboard and help tell the controller which key has been pressed.

The *keyboard input lines* also look for signals from the keyboard. They take the electronic signals to the integrated circuit.

The scan lines and the keyboard input lines are the lookout messengers we mentioned before.

These three parts work together to carry the electronic pulses that take the numbers from the keyboard to the display.

To see how the numbers get from the keyboard to the display, it will help to look at the drawing on page 30. This drawing uses symbols for the parts of the calculator. The large box at the bottom stands for the integrated circuit. The lines are the wires, and the arrows show the direction in which the electric current flows.

The eighteen little blocks in the middle of the drawing stand for the calculator keys. The nine boxes above the keys are the display. Find the segment lines a through h. Find the scan lines and

Before integrated circuits are put onto chips, the designs are plotted out and checked on large sheets of paper.

29

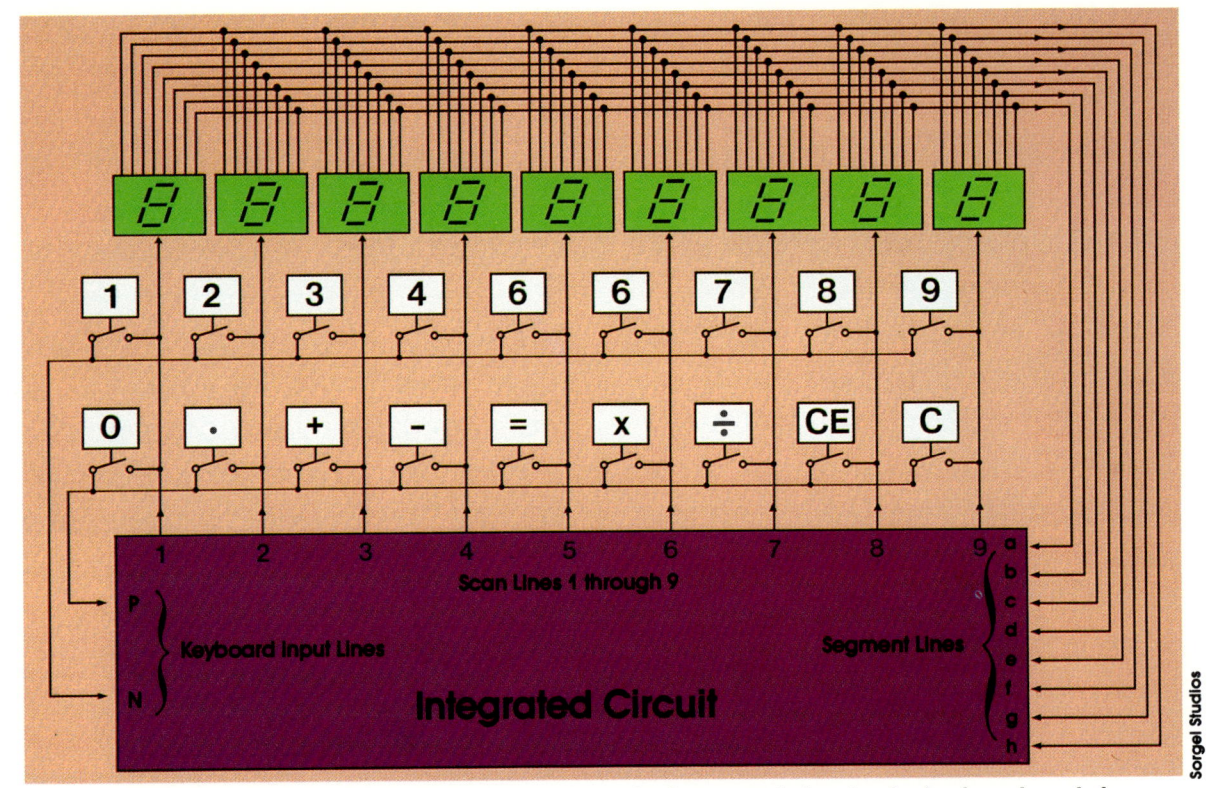

This is a diagram of the various connections among the integrated circuit, the keyboard, and the display. The arrows show the direction of the flow of electricity.

the keyboard input lines. Use your finger to trace the path of the current as we talk about these lines.

When the calculator is on, the integrated circuit continuously sends pulses through the nine scan lines. It sends these pulses over and over again. The controller's clock times the pulses, and they go through the scan lines thousands of times every second.

When you press a key, the integrated circuit gets two signals. One signal comes from one of the scan lines. The other signal comes from one of the keyboard input lines. The integrated circuit checks both the scan lines and the keyboard input lines for messages. For example, when the 3 key is pressed, the integrated circuit gets a message from scan line 3 and also from keyboard input line N.

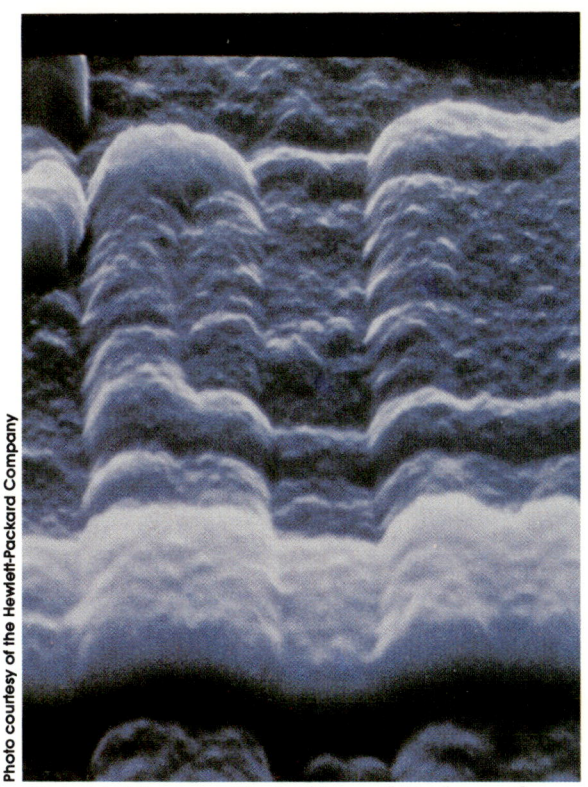

This highly magnified silicon chip shows the layers that form an integrated circuit.

Photo courtesy of the Hewlett-Packard Company

Find these lines on the drawing. You'll see they cross at the number 3. That's how the integrated circuit knows exactly which key has been pressed.

Once the integrated circuit knows which key has been pressed, it sends a message to the display. The display then shows the correct number in the correct character position. The integrated circuit uses the scan lines and segment lines to show a number in the display.

Each scan line is connected to all eight segments in a character position. For example, scan line 4 is connected to all eight segments in character position 4. Notice that the segments and the segment lines are labeled a through h. For a number to light up in the display, the integrated circuit must turn on a scan line as well as the proper segments. For example, when the 1 key is pressed, the integrated circuit turns on scan line 1 and segments b and c. When the 3 key is pressed, the integrated circuit turns on scan line 3 and segments a, b, c, d, and g.

Press the 8 key several times and watch the numbers light up. It looks as if the whole number (that is, all seven segments) appears instantly. Actually, the integrated circuit "builds" the number by turning on one segment at a time. It turns on each segment in order. This action is called *strobing*. Strobing happens more than 200 times each second. Because the

31

electric pulses pass through the segments so fast, it looks as if the segments all light up at the same time.

The instant a number is lit in the display, the integrated circuit again starts scanning and checking the keyboard to see whether another key has been pressed.

A calculator uses a special code in order to send messages from one part to another. This code works with switches and wires. The switches turn electricity on and off in the wires. Which wires are on and which are off determine what message is sent. That is, different wires are on and off for, say, an 8 than are on and off for a 6.

Each calculator key has its own pattern of on-and-off switches. Each key needs four wires to be able to use the special message code. Each of the four wires has a different value. These values are: 8, 4, 2, and 1. In order to send a 2 in our code, the 8, 4, and 1 wires are off, and the 2 wire is on. To send a 5, the 8 and 2 wires are off, and the 4 and 1 wires are on. We then add the values of the "on" wires (that is, 4 and 1) to get 5.

THE BINARY CODE

Let's look at the whole code. First of all, 1 means a switch is on, and 0 means a switch is off. Now let's use the four wires and the switches to represent a 6. Don't forget, the wires have the values 8, 4, 2, and 1. When all four wires are off, we represent them like this: 0000. To send a 6 in the code, we turn on the 4 wire and the 2 wire. That would look like this: 0110. (Remember, in the code, 1 and 0 aren't the numerals one and zero, they are just symbols that mean "on" and "off.") So, we have off-on-on-off. The values of the two "on" wires are 4 and 2—which equals 6.

Today hundreds of thousands of transistors (shown in the background) can be incorporated onto one silicon chip.

Photo courtesy of the Hewlett-Packard Company

Photo courtesy of the Hewlett-Packard Company

Here is a table that shows you the codes for the numbers 0 through 9.

Wire Values: 8421	Decimal Digit	Translation
0000 =	0	(0 + 0 + 0 + 0)
0001 =	1	(0 + 0 + 0 + 1)
0010 =	2	(0 + 0 + 2 + 0)
0011 =	3	(0 + 0 + 2 + 1)
0100 =	4	(0 + 4 + 0 + 0)
0101 =	5	(0 + 4 + 0 + 1)
0110 =	6	(0 + 4 + 2 + 0)
0111 =	7	(0 + 4 + 2 + 1)
1000 =	8	(8 + 0 + 0 + 0)
1001 =	9	(8 + 0 + 0 + 1)

The numbers in this code are called *binary numbers*. Binary means something related to the number two. It is something with two parts. Our code uses only two symbols, 1 and 0. It is a binary code.

Because the binary system is based on the number 2, the value of each wire is multiplied by two to get the value of the next wire. We begin with 1. Then we multiply by 2 to get 2—the second wire. Then 2 is multiplied by 2 to get 4—the value of the third wire.

Finally, 4 is multiplied by 2 to get 8—the fourth wire. To figure the values for more wires, keep multiplying by 2. This is how the calculator breaks numbers into small bits so that it can handle all kinds of problems.

The instrument at the left can test chips on a printed-circuit board at the rate of about thirty each second.

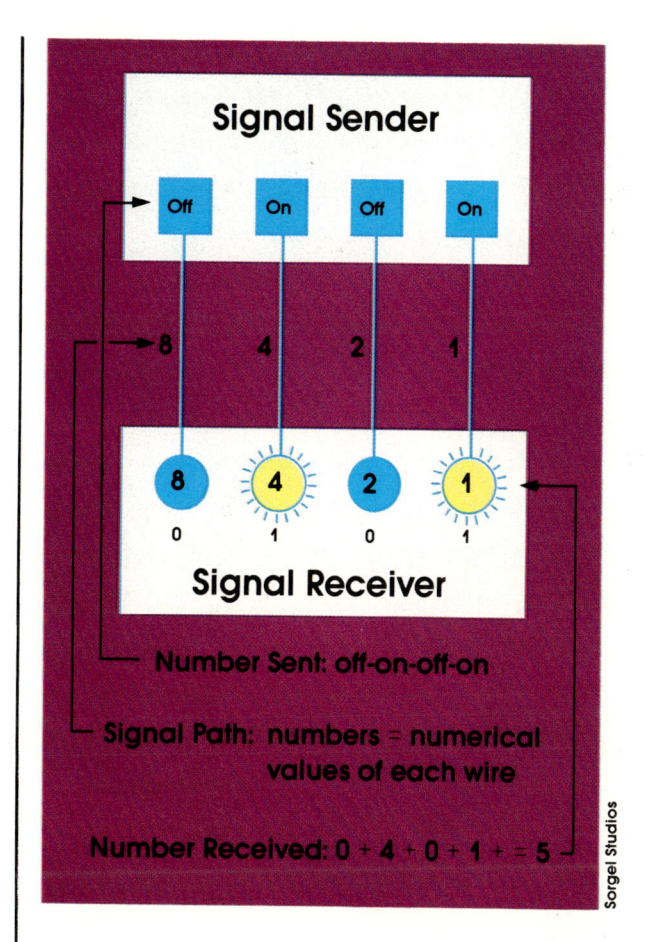

164,950.00
AMORT
INT
NPV
RND
IRR
n
i
PV
PMT
FV
CHS
7
8
9
÷
BEG
END
MEM
DEPRECIATION
SOYD
DB
SL
PRICE
BOND
YTM
%T
Δ%
%
EEX
4
5
6
×
D.MY
M.DY
INTG
FRAC
CLEAR
FIN
REG
PREFIX
1/x
CLX
ENTER
1
2
3
−
P/R
R/S
PRGM
x≷y
0
.
Σ+
+
RCL
ON
DATE
ΔDYS
LSTx
x=0
HEWL

OTHER KINDS OF PROBLEMS

You have seen how a calculator adds numbers. Subtracting is done basically the same way. Except that when a problem goes into the adder-subtracter, it subtracts rather than adds.

But how does a calculator multiply and divide? Just as it does with all operations, a calculator breaks the problem into small parts. A calculator breaks a multiplication problem into a series of small addition problems. How? First, let's change the addition problem we looked at to a multiplication problem: 3 × 5. Another way to think about "three times five" is that we are adding 3 five times. We could say "three plus three plus three plus three plus three." And that's exactly what the calculator does. When you press the ⊞ key in a problem, the lookout messenger simply tells the controller to add the first number to the second number *once*. When you press the ⊠ key, the lookout messenger tells the controller to add the first number as many times as the second number. So in the problem

3 × 5, the calculator actually adds 3 + 3 + 3 + 3 + 3.

Similarly, the calculator breaks a division problem into a series of subtraction problems. Look at the problem 6 ÷ 2. You can think of this as "six divided by two" or as "how many two's are there in six?" One way to find out how many two's there are in six is to keep subtracting 2 from 6 until you end up with zero. You would say 6 − 2 = 4; 4 − 2 = 2; 2 − 2 = 0. You had to subtract 2 from 6 three times. And that's the answer—6 ÷ 2 = 3. Again, that is exactly how the calculator does a division problem. It subtracts 6 − 2 − 2 − 2.

We've covered many ideas about how a calculator works. We've seen how numbers are sent from the keyboard to the integrated circuit. We've talked about where numbers are remembered and saved and how they are added, subtracted, multiplied, and divided. We know how numbers are sent to the display. We've seen how the calculator takes information and breaks it down into very simple terms—to questions of yes or no, on or off. We've also discovered that the calculator uses the binary number system to handle information.

We have said several times that calculators work almost like magic. And in many ways they do. However, calculators only work their magic because people have told them how. An integrated circuit or a controller or a chip couldn't do anything unless people programmed them. Programs are the permanent instructions in certain calculator parts. For example, in order for a calculator to give the answer 8 for the problem 3 + 5, people must first program the controller and the adder-subtracter to do so. A person *could* program a calculator to give the answer 4,627 to the problem 3 + 5. But that wouldn't make sense, and it wouldn't be helpful. And it certainly wouldn't be very good magic.

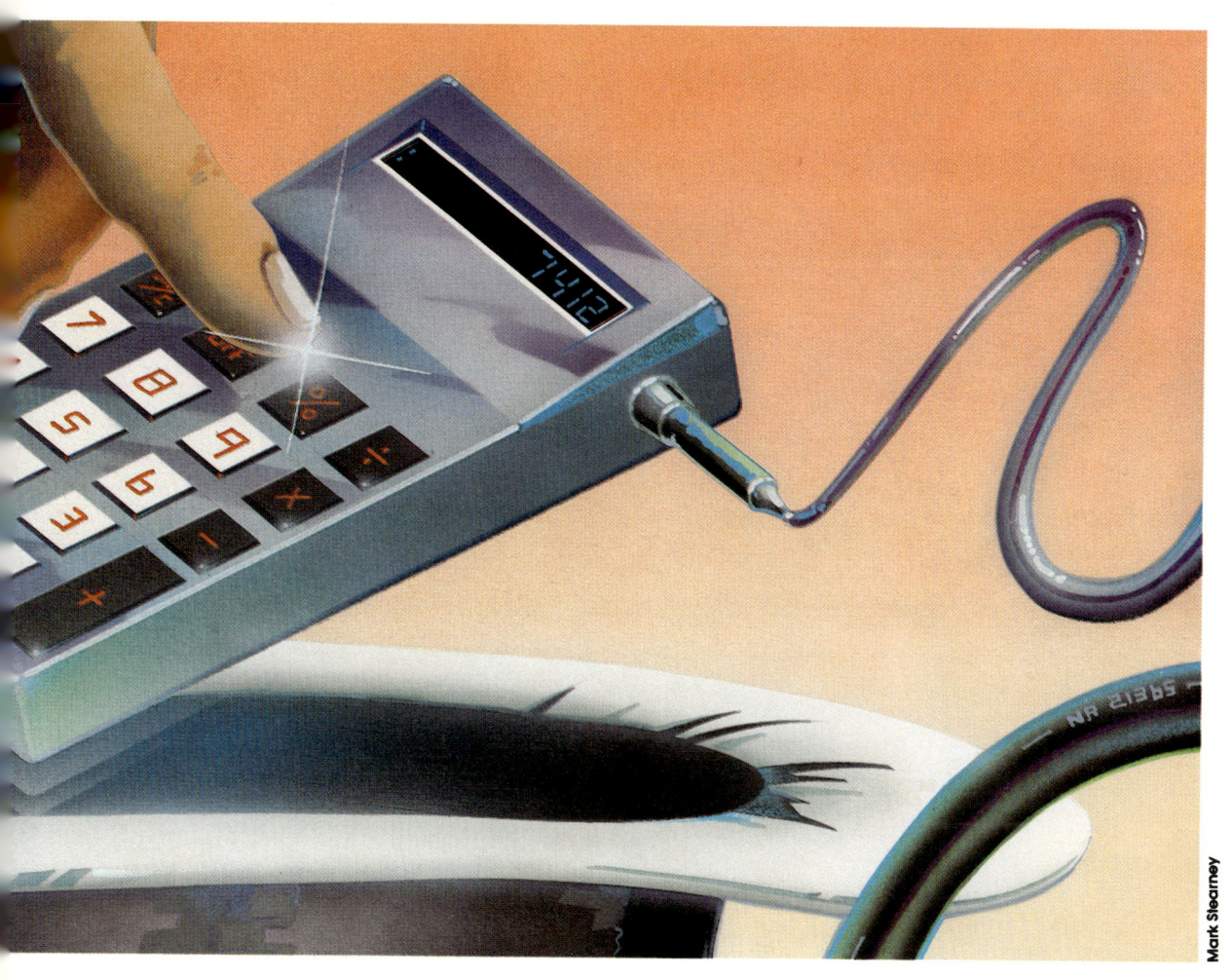

HEWLETT·PACKARD 67
W/PRGM
RUN
ENTER
LUNAR POSITION
ARITHMETIC TEACHER
SD-13A
TABULATOR
SD-02A
MOVING AVERAGE
SD-01A
POLYNOMIAL EVALUATION
SD-09A
CURVE FITTING
SD-03A
SD-07A
ANNUITIES AND COMPOUND AMOUNTS
SD-05A

PLAYING WITH NUMBERS

All the parts of a calculator work together in a certain order to make the calculator a powerful tool. Handheld calculators do arithmetic quickly and accurately. But calculators are not only for work. Most people have found calculators can be great fun to play with. The same things are happening inside calculators whether you use them for solving problems or for games and puzzles. In this section we'll explore some of the fun you can have with your calculator.

Flip-it Puzzles

When you look at the display upside down, some of the numbers look like letters. With a little imagination you can see that the following numbers correspond to the letters shown when the calculator is "flipped":

0 = O	5 = S
1 = I	6 = g
2 = Z	7 = L
3 = E	8 = B
4 = h	9 = G

(The "letters" Z, g, B, and G are often tougher to "see"—until you

A special program card can convert this calculator into a game calculator.

41

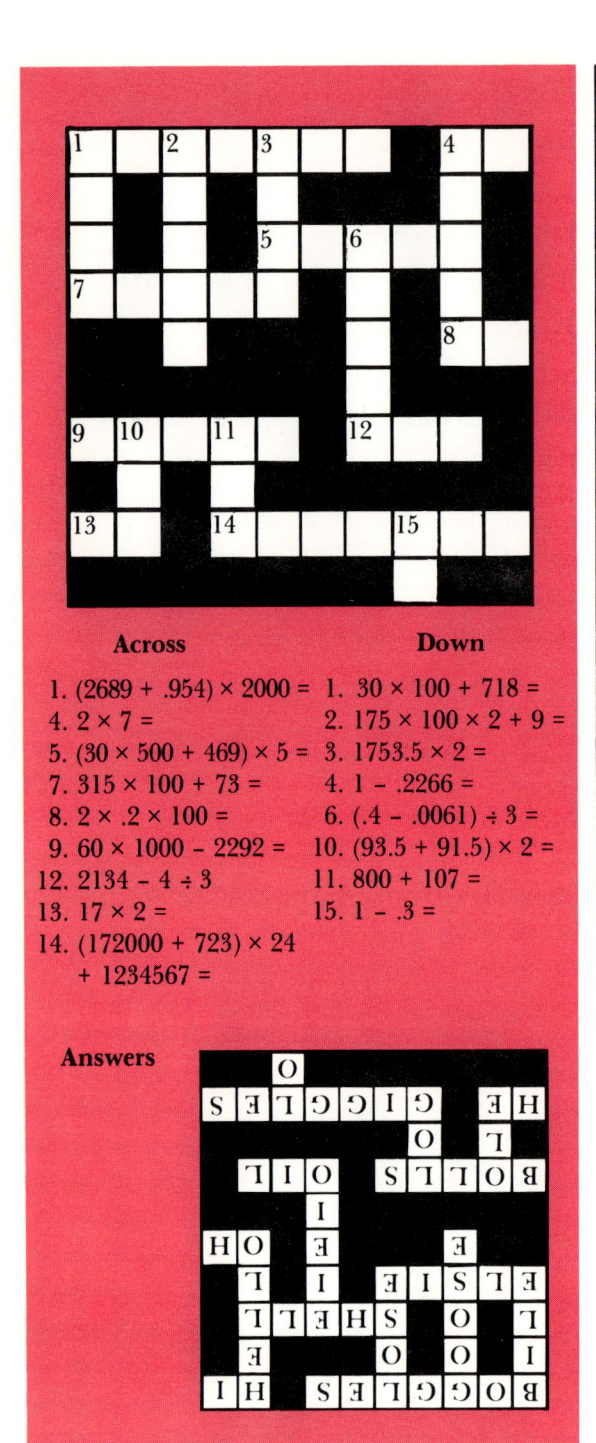

get used to them.) Try these problems, turn the calculator around, and work this crossword puzzle.

Magicalc

Amaze your friends with this mathematical trick! Hand a friend your calculator. Your friend keys a favorite three-digit number. Then have your friend:

a) Repeat the digits, making a six-digit number.

b) Say that your magical power tells you that the number can be divided by 13. Have your friend press ➗ 13 ＝.

c) Now you "feel" the result can be divided by 11. Have your friend key in ➗ 11 ＝. Once again you're right.

d) Now that you've gone through divisions by "unlucky" 13 and the magic number 11, you make a final suggestion. Have your friend key in ➗ 7 ＝. And . . . back comes the original number—unharmed after all those divisions.

Gotcha!

Gotcha! is a calculator game for two or more players that can be

Across

1. (2689 + .954) × 2000 =
4. 2 × 7 =
5. (30 × 500 + 469) × 5 =
7. 315 × 100 + 73 =
8. 2 × .2 × 100 =
9. 60 × 1000 − 2292 =
12. 2134 − 4 ÷ 3
13. 17 × 2 =
14. (172000 + 723) × 24 + 1234567 =

Down

1. 30 × 100 + 718 =
2. 175 × 100 × 2 + 9 =
3. 1753.5 × 2 =
4. 1 − .2266 =
6. (.4 − .0061) ÷ 3 =
10. (93.5 + 91.5) × 2 =
11. 800 + 107 =
15. 1 − .3 =

Answers

played anywhere you've got your calculator (in your car, while camping, etc.).

Player 1 enters 50 into the display and then secretly presses one of the operation keys: ⊞, ⊟, ⊠, or ⊡. Then Player 1 passes the calculator to the next player.

Player 2 must then enter any number (except 1) and press ⊜.

If the display shows a negative number, a number over 200, or "Error," Player 2 loses and must the leave game.

If the display shows a number between 0 and 200, player 2 then secretly presses ⊞, ⊟, ⊠, or ⊡ and passes the calculator, and the game goes on.

The game is over when only one player is left—the winner!

Hexagon 38

Your calculator and some logical thinking make this next puzzle fun. Fill in each hexagon below with numbers from 1 to 19, in such a way that all the numbers along any straight line add up to 38. (Don't use any of the numbers more than once.) A few have been put in to help out.

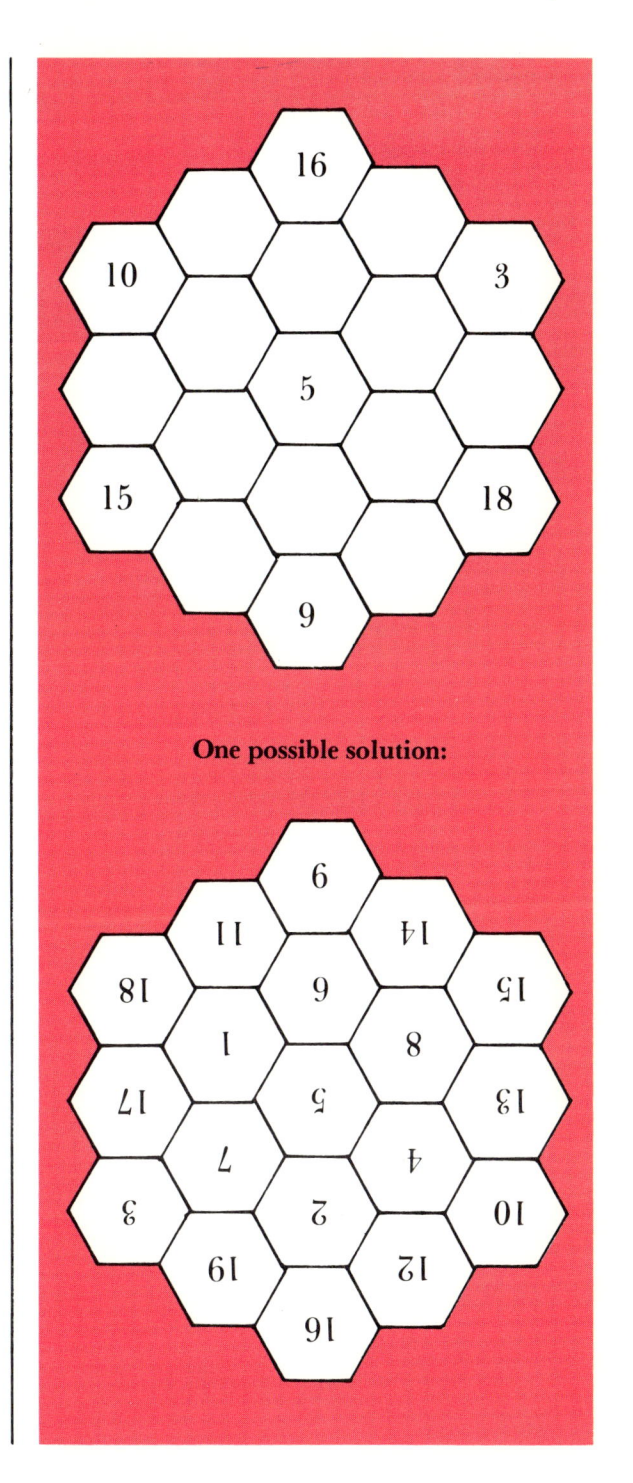

[Hexagonal puzzle grid with numbers: 16, 10, 3, 5, 15, 18, 9]

One possible solution:

[Hexagonal grid solution shown upside down with numbers: 9, 11, 14, 18, 6, 15, 1, 8, 17, 5, 13, 3, 7, 4, 10, 19, 2, 12, 16]

43

Numbers, Life, the Universe, and You!

With your calculator, you can explore some of the numbers in the world around you. Here are some questions with interesting answers you can calculate. Then think up a few of your own!

Life Questions:

• How many times has your heart beat since you were born?
Solution: Get a watch and count your pulse for one minute. Then do this calculation: Pulse rate (beats per minute) × 60 × 24 × 365 × (your age) = total number of heartbeats.

A person breathes as much air in one year as there is in about five gas balloons.

• How many Saturday nights are there until you're 100? (Assume a long life!)
Solution: (100 − your age) × 52 = ___. Ever thought about that?

• How much air do you breathe in a year?
Solution: Your lungs breathe in about .47 liters (1 pt) of air at a time. Check your number of breaths per minute with a watch (that's tricky to do). Then: number of breaths per minute × .47 × 60 × 24 × 365 = ___.

PRONUNCIATION GUIDE

These symbols have the same sounds as the darker letters in the sample words.

ə	b**a**lloon, **a**go
a	m**a**p, h**a**ve
ä	f**a**ther, c**a**r
b	**b**all, ri**b**
d	**d**id, a**dd**
e	b**e**ll, g**e**t
ē	k**ee**n, l**ea**p
f	**f**an, so**f**t
g	**g**ood, bi**g**
h	**h**urt, a**h**ead
i	r**i**p, **i**ll
ī	s**i**de, sk**y**
j	**j**oin, **g**erm
k	**k**ing, as**k**
l	**l**et, coo**l**
m	**m**an, sa**m**e
n	**n**o, tur**n**
ō	c**o**ne, kn**ow**
ȯ	**a**ll, s**aw**
p	**p**art, scra**p**
r	**r**oot, ti**r**e
s	**s**o, pre**ss**
sh	**sh**oot, ma**ch**ine
t	**t**o, s**t**and
ü	p**oo**l, l**o**se
ů	p**u**t, b**oo**k
v	**v**iew, gi**v**e
w	**w**ood, glo**w**ing
y	**y**es, **y**ear
′	accent

GLOSSARY

These words are defined the way they used in the book.

abacus (ab′ ə kəs) the first calculating device, invented about 5,000 years ago

adder-subtracter (ad′ ər səb trak′ tər) the part of a calculator that figures out all the answers to the problems a calculator does

binary system (bī′ nə rē sis′ təm) a number system, based on the number 2, that uses only the symbols 1 and 0

chip (chip) a tiny piece of silicon that holds all the electronics that make a calculator operate

circuit (electric) (sər′ kət) the path of electric current

computer (kəm pyü′ tər) an electronic device that can be programmed and can store, retrieve, and process information

controller (kən trō′ lər) the part of a calculator that directs most of the operations that go on in a calculator

display (dis plā′) the window at the top of a calculator, which shows numbers after keys have been pressed

instruction messengers (in strək′ shən mes′ ən jərz) pulses of electric

45

current that gather information in the calculator and then tell the controller what needs to be done

integrated circuit (IC) (int′ ə grā təd sər′ kət) the part of a calculator where all the paths of electricity are

keyboard (kē′ bȯrd) the group of keys on a calculator

keyboard input lines (kē′ bȯrd in′ pu̇t līnz) circuits that work with scan lines to watch for signals coming from the keyboard and that take those signals to the controller; also called, in this book, lookout messengers

lookout messengers (lu̇k′ au̇t mes′ ən jərz) pulses of electric current that gather information from the keyboard and then tell the controller what needs to be done

memory (mem′ ə rē) parts of a calculator in which numbers or operations (such as "add," "subtract," etc.) can be saved

memory box messenger (mem′ ə rē bäks mes′ ən jər) pulses of electric current that move numbers in and out of a calculator's memory

number position (nəm′ bər pə zish′ ən) the section in a calculator's display where a single number lights up

printed-circuit board (print′ əd sər′ kət bȯrd) a board that holds a calculator's display, integrated circuit, and printed circuits

scan lines (skan′ līnz) circuits that work with keyboard input lines to watch for signals coming from the keyboard and that take those signals to the controller; also called, in this book, lookout messengers

segment line (seg′ mənt līn) a circuit that carries electricity through the number segments and light a number in the display

segments (number) (seg′ məntz) the small lights that form numbers in the display

silicon (sil′ i kən) a hard, metallike material of which a calculator's chip is made

terminal (tər′ mən əl) the metal pins through which electricity goes in and out of an integrated circuit

INDEX

abacus, 6
adder-subtracter, 26, 37, 39
addition, 24-26, 37-38
answer memory box, 26
binary code, 32-35
binary number, 35
binary system, 35
character position, 31
chip, 16-17, 29, 39
circuit (electric), 14
clock (calculator), 20
computer, 8, 15
controller, 19, 20, 23-24, 26, 29, 30, 37-38, 39
counting, 5
currrent (electric), 19, 26, 29, 30
display, 11-12, 20, 23, 24, 26, 27, 29, 31, 32, 38
display messenger, 20, 23-24, 26
division, 37-38
games, 41-44
Hollerith, Herman, 8
instruction messenger, 19
instructions, 19
integrated circuit (IC), 14, 16, 17-19, 20, 26, 29, 30, 31, 32, 38, 39
key (calculator), 11, 29, 32
keyboard, 11, 13, 20, 23, 24, 29, 32, 38
keyboard input line, 13, 29-31
laser beam, 29
lookout messenger, 20, 23, 24, 29, 37-38
mathematics, 5-6
memory, 20

memory box, 23-24
memory box, "waiting," 24
memory-box messenger, 20, 23-24
messages, 19
multiplication, 37-38
Napier, John, 6-7
Napier's Bones, 7
negative number, 27
number position, 27, 29
Pascal, Blaise, 7
power source, 11
printed-circuit board, 13, 29
program, 39
punch card, 8
puzzles, 41-44
scan line, 29-31
segment (number), 27, 29, 31-32
segment line, 29-31
silicon, 16
subtraction, 37-38
switches, on-and-off, 32
terminal, 15-16
wires, 29, 32
X-ray, 29